Step With the OTHER Left Foot

Step With the OTHER Left Foot

Step With the Other Left Foot-a book of drills, tips, and silly stories that can be used and enjoyed by anyone who loves to play the game of tennis

MELISSA KELLY

Illustrations by Stacy Bates
Court Illustrations by Stacey Glover

ISBN-13: 9780692071786
ISBN-10: 0692071784

Table of Contents

Foreword

This Ones for the Ladies

Tennis has been a huge part of over half my life. Most of that has been spent coaching. I have coached some very good players over the years as well as some players who were not quite as gifted, but still played the game with the same fervor

I feel like a very well- rounded coach. I can teach a 3-year-old girl whose most urgent tennis need is to get another cup of water or an 80-year-old man who doesn't want to waste a single minute of his lesson time and just wants to hit. I must admit, though, that my favorite lessons involve the ladies. You know who I'm talking about. The ones who show up to drop their kids off at school in their tennis skirt. The ones who race from their desk at lunch to go get in a 45-minute cardio tennis class. That lady with the killer tan and a match every night? She is one of them. I'm going to be the one to say it. These ladies are the life blood of tennis.

That's right. Not Johnny Junior and his killer forehand. These ladies are what drives the tennis train, people. It's time they were given their dues.

It's not saying that all the other players in this crazy world of tennis aren't important. We need the Federer's and Serena's to give us something to dream about. We need those ex- college players to show us what we would look like if we had just started earlier. And, honestly, there is nothing more adorable than 8 and Under tennis. Let's face it, the odds of Johnny Junior playing college tennis are slim. I always have a few juniors who have a good chance to play collegiately, but sometimes life takes them another direction. Even if Johnny Junior plays all the way through 18's, he is more than likely going to drop lessons with his pro the day he leaves for college. Various pros taught Johnny all the way until he left the nest to begin a new chapter in his life, and now it's just another slot to fill. If they were lucky, they taught him for about 6 good years and now he is just a fading memory. This is just how the cycle works.

His mom is a different story. You got her started in Tennis for $20 (4 group lessons for $20, how can she say no???) She quickly became addicted. She starts playing daily, sometimes several times a day. Then the time comes to join or form a team. In one year, she learns the basics of the game and you soon learn that she is playing on 4 different teams during the spring season. She buys racquets, shoes, matching team out-fits, grips, strings, and lessons. She progresses through the NTRP system and plays on about 10 teams that year. She plays more matches than Serena and Federer combined.

She deserves our respect.

Respect. I have watched pros over the years disrespect this demographic over and over. She's just a woman so let her hit it any way she wants to. If she is a housewife, money is no object and her time is not valuable. She's just a woman so I will not teach her any technique because she is not capable. She is just a woman, so she can just get the serve in to start the point.

To all the pros who say this daily, you are lazy, sexist, and have no clue.

I said it. I have seen this over and over in this and other industries. They are taken for granted and treated like they aren't capable. I have news for you. These ladies are, for the most part, well-educated and probably hold or held a pretty damn good job (probably making more than you!) If they are a housewife, they were attractive and intelligent enough to land a well-off spouse and not have to go back to work. Some ladies could stay home, but choose to work. Some of them work hard to pay their bills and tennis is their luxury. They spend their days devoted to their children and families and they always get asked, and are expected, to volunteer. Home room mom? That's her, and she brought donuts. Fundraiser? She helps organize it and brings in donations. Her volunteer hours are almost the equivalent of a full-time job!

Someone once asked me about my favorite coaching experience. I didn't have to think very long. It's getting the call. You know the one. "Hi, my name is Julie, I got your number from so and so. I have never played before and I would really like to get in some lessons to try it out." That takes guts, people. Some are former athletes, but a lot have never played a sport. Like, ever! To show up at a tennis court with no experience and start to learn a game that is insanely difficult???? As an adult????? My hats off to you. All of you. How many of you tennis pros branch out and take on new experiences, not athletic? Maybe guitar, or painting, or cooking? It's hard when you are so good at something to remember not being good at it. Most of us don't try new things because we don't want to be terrible at it. These ladies just walked to the edge of the cliff and jumped into the tennis abyss.

This book of drills, tips, and silly stories can be used and enjoyed by anyone who loves to play, but, as I said at the beginning, this one's for the ladies...

One

The Art, and Sometimes Comedy, of Serving

Me:"Don't chase your toss"
My lesson:"Yeah, but I don't want to waste it"

The Second Serve Blues

I have some wonderful news for all of you! No matter what level you get to, ladies, the second serve will pretty much always suck! I am not making this up! Yeah, there will be the occasional lady with a big kicker or the one with no difference between their first and second serve, but this is very rare. Most ladies just get it in. You know who you are. Right now, most of you are nodding and laughing because not only do you do it, you have said those four words to somebody somewhere: "Just get it in" (get your mind out of the gutter!). These words are the worst four words in tennis. They pretty much guarantee you a terrible, poopy, awful looking second serve.

Every time one of my ladies comes to a lesson and starts bragging that she didn't have any double faults, I cringe. You better not double fault at all with that 3 mph second serve, girl!!!!

First things first. Tell your pro you want to learn the real thing. You want a loop, the right grip, the works! Your pro should not assume that you are not capable of learning this. You can do this! Have you already been playing for years and find it's really hard to change? You're right. It is incredibly hard to change! Learn it right from the beginning and your entire tennis life will be much more fun and rewarding. There is still hope for you, my tennis veterans with tough to break bad habits, and we will get back to that.

The Grip

There is no debate here if you want a good 1st and 2nd serve. You must use the hammer grip (otherwise known as the continental, but hammer is easier to remember). This grip will help keep the racquet face closed (facing the ground) on the back swing so it will give you a little more leeway if you hit the ball a little late or early. If you have the wrong grip (frying pan) your strings are wide open on the back swing, so you better hit that sucker right on time if you want to hit it with pace and get it in. Or you can just hit it 3 mph to know you will get it in...

Do you have the wrong grip and want to change it? You have a couple of options... Go cold turkey and change to the hammer grip no matter what. No matter what peer pressure you face, even from Ms. "Just get it in", don't go back to the old ways. The other is a gradual shift. Over the course of a few months, just move it a smidge (that is a technical term). Eventually, you will achieve grip nirvana.

The Motion

When it comes to mechanics, I do feel there is more than one way to skin a cat (isn't that the most disgusting saying?). However, there are still fundamentals we need to have. I am going to cover the basic service motion. Once you master it, feel free to put your own spin to it, pun intended.

 Don't worry about your feet right now! Just keep still for a bit!

First, if you are right handed, point your left foot towards the right net post. This should help ensure your body is properly turned. Yes, you do this on both the deuce and the ad side. Start the racquet strings and the ball out in front of you. Make sure the ball and the strings are touching. This will ensure this part stays consistent. Next, bring the racquet arm and the toss up at the same time to make a "Y". Do this several times. You should be able to catch the ball in your tossing hand without moving your feet.

Now, put that ball in your pocket. This is about to get real in a hurry.

Make the "Y" and practice looping your racquet arm. It's like throwing a lasso, because we are all so good throwing lassos. You can also pretend like you are going to throw your racquet over the net. Don't forget that left tossing arm in all of this. When the racquet arm goes back up to hit the ball, the tossing hand goes down to your left hip. A good way to practice looping is to get a tube sock (just watch some movies from the 70's and you will see lots of tube socks) and put about 6-8 tennis balls in it. Now practice serving with it. If you don't loop correctly, you will get nailed with a giant sock full of balls. Good times.

Now, get that ball out of your pocket.

Time to practice the motion with the ball. We are usually pretty good until we add the ball into the equation. Just keep practicing. You do not look like an idiot. You look like someone trying to learn tennis the correct way.

The "F" Word (Footwork)

You can't spend hours on your strokes and ignore your footwork. If you have Serena strokes, but you don't have Serena footwork, you will not look like Serena. True story.

Footwork on the serve is as easy as it gets! You are tossing the ball as opposed to the ball coming towards you with random spins and speeds. That means you have more time to think about what you are doing. There are a few different options for you to choose from when it comes to footwork. You can bring your feet together and jump, keep them apart and jump, or just let that right leg swing in the court. Just remember, these happen because you are swinging up and forward. The easiest of the three is just to let your right leg swing forward. Your racquet is going forward so you go forward. Easy as that. Whichever footwork you choose, just remember to toss before you bend. Don't bend then toss! You will end up with your toss all over the place! If you look at the illustration above, you will see an example of bringing the feet together for the knee bend. If my client wants an explosive serve, this is my favorite method to teach. When the feet are together, it is more difficult for them to chase their toss as opposed to the feet staying apart through the knee bend. Either stance is correct, this is just my preference!

The Toss

Struggling with the toss? That's ok and that is very normal! Think about how much control you have when you write or throw a ball with your non-dominate hand. It's not much! This is something worth spending some of your practice time on. If your toss is terrible, you will struggle with the consistency of your serve.

There are many ways to practice the toss. One of the first methods I like to use is to have my student stand a foot or two away from one the fences. They begin with the racquet back behind their head and facing at the same angle away from the fence as they would begin a serve behind the baseline. Have them toss the ball up and swing the racquet towards the fence so that it traps the ball between the racquet and the fence. Not only will this show them how high or low their point of contact is, it will also help them find the optimal tossing location.

Another method I like to use is to have the student line up in the proper stance behind the baseline like they are preparing to serve. I then have them place the racquet on the ground with the butt cap of the racquet touching the toe box of their left shoe and the tip of the racquet head pointed toward the right net post. I then have them toss the ball with their left hand about three to four feet above their head and let it drop to the ground. Don't let them catch it! The goal is for the ball to bounce on or around the racquet strings on the ground. If you don't think they are getting that toss up high enough (or if it is too high!), stand in front of them with your racquet held up (imitating point of contact on their serve). This will give them a better gauge how high that toss needs to be.

Two

The Easy Overhead

Me: "What's the first thing you think of
when a lob goes up in the air?"
My Lesson: "Well, shit"

The Easy Overhead

Ah, the easy overhead. Nothing gives you a feeling of greater satisfaction or absolute agony like this shot. You literally played the entire point for this moment. You made amazing digs, great gets, and an amazing defensive lob. This is your moment. You are just 5 feet from the net. The ball is floating towards you like a beach ball at a concert. The easiest shot you could possibly get after playing such a tough point.

Annnnnnnd, you blow it!

WTH? How does this happen? How could you miss the easiest shot you will ever get? This is 100 percent mental. Technique is important here and so is the grip, but even with these two fundamentals, you can still miss it. I tell my students that one of two things go through your head when the easy overhead goes up. You are either the type that sees it and thinks "Come to Momma!" or, you are like most of us, and think "Don't miss it, don't miss it". If you are the latter of the two, you are pretty much set up for failure.

Part of the problem here is we don't practice it enough. You aren't getting enough reps to be confident about making the shot. How much do you practice your overhead? Most people only practice the overhead in the 5-10-minute warmup before the match. So, if they are lucky, they practice about 3-5 overheads. This is not enough! Not even close. Give your overhead the same attention as you would your volley or your backhand for one month. You will be shocked at how much better your overhead gets.

Technical Stuff

No, I am not letting you off the hook with that terrible, frying pan grip. Now that we have conquered the mental aspect of the overhead, let's talk turkey. The overhead uses, wait for it, wait for it…the hammer grip! Get used to this. Everything but your forehand ground stroke uses this grip. I know this is just what you wanted to hear! As far as the actual swing, just remember to get the racquet back behind your head, left hand pointing up at the contact point, and swing up and forward. The finish should be on your left side. Prepare that racquet and put that left hand up before you move one step. The earlier you prepare, the more efficient your footwork will be.

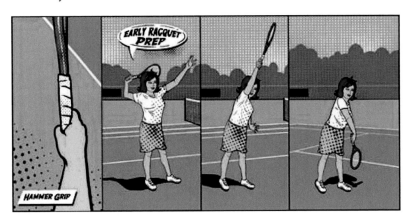

Three

THE FOREHAND

Me: "Make sure you follow through"
My Lesson: "Ugghhh, between you and my
therapist, I can't catch a break"

The Grip

There are actually several grips that can be used for the forehand, but I try to stay neutral on this one. Very Goldilocks and the Three Bears. The one in the middle is just right. This grip is formally called a semi-western, but I like to call it the pick off the ground grip. Just put the racquet on the ground directly in front of you, pick it up, and Voila! You have the grip we want. Not everything in tennis is impossibly hard!

Technique

You have a couple of options on the back swing of your forehand. You can either take it straight back and down or you can learn to loop. I am a fan of the loop. You can generate more spin and pace with less effort. I love to get more for less, don't you?

What is a loop? A loop is just a circle or semi-circle. Just a little round thing you do before you hit the ball. I still use a hula hoop for this one. You go above the hula hoop, behind the hula hoop, below the hula hoop, and swing up the front of the hula hoop. I stand there and hold the hula hoop and bounce the ball and my lesson swings. If you don't have anyone willing to stand this dangerously close to you (you need new friends!), just visualize all the parts of the swing.

After you make contact, you still have some work to do. This one kills me. You have this magnificent ground stroke and then you stop the racquet just after contact. That racquet wants to follow through, even if you don't! Let it go where it is destined to go. Finish palm out next to the shoulder. That also means the side of the strings that contacted the ball finishes away from your body.

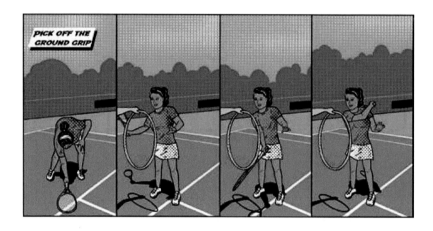

Footwork

I can't stress this enough. You don't step and hit anymore on your forehand and backhand groundstrokes. That is so 1970's. The strike zone was lower then. It is much higher now. Nowadays, we load. Loading is simple. If you are swinging low to high, your legs should go low to high as well. If you are swinging from your back to front, your swing should go from your back foot to front foot. Don't complicate this!

Should you use open stance or closed stance? This is the debate of legends. I am privy to open stance, but I still think closed (or power) stance has its merits. As the game has developed with more power and even more spin, I think open stance is just easier and more efficient most of the time. Closed stance takes a little more time and footwork preparation so if you see me in this stance, I am about to crush your hopes and dreams down the line, sister.

Four

*Me:"What do you do when your opponent
starts picking on your backhand?"
My Lesson:"I run around and hit my forehand"*

Technique (and footwork and strike zone and the meaning of life)

Please, please, please, quit treating your backhand like it's your groom's ex-girlfriend who crashed your wedding. It's not that bad! It's actually much easier than the forehand! I am not against a one handed back hand, but it's so difficult to properly execute, it's just not a viable option for most of us normal people. So, we will just cover the two hander.

Once again, we need to cover that grip. Put the racquet down in front of you and pick it up with the left hand. Make sure you pick it up towards the top of the grip closer to the throat of the racquet. Now grab the grip with your right hand in the hammer position. This grip will not go away, so just drink the hammer Kool-Aid. To loop or not to loop is a very good question. I prefer to teach a straight back swing on the back hand, but a loop can be just as effective. If you loop, just trace a baby hula hoop. If you take a straight backswing, just point the tip of the racquet down towards the bottom of the fence behind you. Ta Da! You look like you should be on tv playing tennis right now.

Now, swing forward. Just let the racquet handle finish next to your right shoulder. Remember, you should swing low to high while moving your legs low to high. Because you have less reach on a two-handed back hand, you will usually need to swing the left leg around for balance and a full hip turn after the follow through.

One little tip for developing a killer back hand. Go get it! Don't let this sucker drop out of the strike zone (strike zone is between the waist and the shoulder). Take it a half to a full step earlier than you think you should. The biggest advantage of hitting a two-handed back hand as opposed to a one handed back hand (other than being a hell of a lot easier!) is you can take the ball earlier yet still be in a comfortable strike zone. Take this advantage and run with it.

Five

THE VOLLEY

Me:"Step with the left foot on the forehand volley"
My Lesson "How was that?"
Me:"The other left foot"

Grip

Let's start with the grip for the forehand and backhand volley. It's a hammer grip. For both shots. You simply will not have enough time to change from one grip to the other while you are at the net (there are other reasons, but I feel like this one should be enough). Balls are flying at your face (again, get your mind out of the gutter). Better have the same grip on both shots so you can protect that dazzling smile and eagle eye vision.

The Forehand Volley Technique

First things first. This is not a swinging volley. This is just a good old, vanilla, basic forehand volley. Don't swing on these volleys? Did you hear me? I'm not playing around with you.

Prepare the racquet as soon as the "F" in forehand volley registers in your brain. Have that racquet just sitting there, completely still, and ready to go. Preparation should be:

1. Racquet head eye level
2. Tip of the racquet head pointed toward the top of the fence behind you
3. Racquet head should be slightly tilted away from your face

You should have a little bit of backswing on a volley. The racquet head should be level with your right ear. It's not a big backswing but enough so you can actually hit it towards the target, not block it. Don't start the racquet so far out in front you can't get anything on it. Your shoulder is responsible for the entire swing. Not your wrist or your elbow. Lock the wrist up and enjoy the experience of the simple volley. Easy and effective. Now take the racquet strings forward towards the target making contact out in front of your left foot. Boom. Look at that thing of beauty. Start the strings towards the target, finish the strings towards the target.

The Backhand Volley Technique

The backhand volley is not very different from everything written above. Pull the racquet back into the prepared position even with your left ear. The left hand should be towards the top of the throat at this point. Keeping that wrist locked, take the racquet forward and make contact out in front of the right foot.

I'm sorry? You want to hit a two-handed back hand volley? That's great! Unfortunately, you will still have to be able to use just one hand sometimes (well, a lot actually). I just don't see the point in learning two different backhand volleys. Tennis has enough to learn as it is without making it more complicated than it should be. If you insist on hitting a two- handed backhand volley, just remember you are sacrificing reach. This is a big sacrifice. This means it is going to require more footwork to get into position to hit the ball. Again, remember to start the strings towards the target and finish the strings towards the target!

Footwork

Volleys are a two-step process (yes, you might have to take more steps to get to the ball, but we will cover your contact footwork here). For the forehand volley, you prepare the racquet, and step towards the racquet with the right foot and step towards the net with the left. Visa versa on the backhand. If you have time to move towards the ball, you have time to prepare. The earlier you prepare, the less likely you are to swing at the volley.

Little tip that I love to use on the volley. You get what you commit to. If you drop your racquet head low, you will let the ball drop to that level. If you put your racquet head up higher, you will move your feet and go get the ball at that level. It's a pretty amazing thing when you force yourself to go get it instead of waiting. This could turn you into a full out net beast.

The Rules of Engagement

1. Lob gets a lob
2. Angle gets an angle
3. Short ball gets a short ball

Lefty Lucy

To all the lefties out there who are just sooooo upset that I have catered this book to the right-handed player: Get over it. The greatest weapon in all of tennis is being a lefty. You could call out "hey, I'm going to slice this out wide every time on the ad side" and it would work. You might have to reverse all my tips and instructions, but us righties must develop a well-rounded service game. You just get to slice and dice us to death.

Yeah, I know scissors are a challenge and the smudge you get on your hand while writing must suck, but we just can't duplicate your leftiness in tennis. Your backhand is your forehand and your forehand is your backhand and your serve spins the wrong way. It's like you are a witch or something.

Six

The Big Three: Basic Doubles Positions

Me:"What's your strategy?"
My Lesson:"Are you going to ask me this every week?"

The Big Three

There are three basic positions in doubles. You have two up, two back, and one up one back. Simple stuff. All three have their merits and you will need to be able to play all three positions (sometimes, you could be in all three positions during one point. Pretty kinky stuff!). Let's start with the most common position, one up and one back.

One Up, One Back

By far the most popular position and, without a doubt, the most boring and least effective. One up and one back consists of two players going at it cross court with some groundstrokes from the baseline while their poor partners are shifting themselves to death in a desperate attempt to poach one out of 100 balls. If you are way more consistent from the baseline than the other person, go for it. You half court singles the hell out of that match. A lot of players tell me they play back while their partner plays up. This isn't really a thing. It's one thing to prefer one or the other, but you still need to be able to do both.

If you insist on playing this way (I get it, we have all been here), you need to understand how you chose which side you are going to play on. Why (all my righties) do you choose to play the deuce side? Because you love that big girl forehand of yours. It's your pride and joy. You have birthday parties for it and tell it how awesome it is. It's the baby. What you need to understand is that is why your opponent is playing that side as well. If her baby is bigger than your baby, then Houston, we have a problem. You are going to have to find the right amount of depth (whether short enough, angled enough, or deep enough) to stay in that rally from the baseline. If you leave that ball between the service line and the 10 and Under baseline, she is going to unleash the beast on you and your partner.

If you play the ad side…think about how you ended up a specialist on this side. When you first got started, they asked which side you wanted to play. One lady said "Forehand side! (this is slang for deuce. Every lefty just rolled their eyes). Then, you uttered those fateful words, "I can play either", and your ad side career took off. Just. Like. That. In my glory days, I played this side. I loved it. Poaching was easier, and I loved the inside out forehand. Most importantly, however, I loved knowing that, ad in or ad out, the game was on my shoulders. I wouldn't have it any other way. If you or your partner is uncomfortable with the responsibility of the ad in or ad out point, it might warrant switching return sides. Tennis is 90 percent mental, so don't underrate this point!

Shifting One Up, One Back

Remember I said the poor net person was shifting themselves to death? Now we are getting to that part. Whenever the back person on your opponent's side has the ball the opposite net person (you) is up inside the service box and looking at them. When they inevitably hit the ball by you and you can't get it, you shift back towards the "t" and look at the other net person. Don't look back! If you keep your eyes forward, you will know exactly how awesome or how terrible of a shot your partner has hit. This can go on forever without the net person touching a single ball. I would rather watch grass grow.

Two Up

My favorite. When you are two up, you are dictating play. I am not guaranteeing you a win, here, but you are at least in control. Now, let me dispel a vicious rumor and myth that permeates all of tennis.

The forehand takes the middle. Totally true if you have tons of time to communicate. If I have time to say, "I've got it" then I have time to invade your space and take that ball with my forehand. The rest of the time, it is not true. Whoever is crosscourt from the person hitting the ball takes the middle. It is their duty. When you have a little Serena Junior over their blasting forehand groundstrokes or volleys at lightning speed down the middle, the ball is traveling at an angle towards the cross-court person who is up. Backhand, forehand, whatever, you need to be there. If you are cross court from the person hitting the ball, you are also the closer. That means you are the number one beast. Close one step per volley towards that center net strap. Don't come crashing in like a wild banshee. Slow your roll and close the net like you are hitting beach balls, not marbles.

The up person down the line from the person hitting the ball is the stagger. Their first responsibility is covering their line, and their second responsibility is covering all lobs that make it over either their head or your head. I see two partners come in together all the time, but they stall on the service line. This is why! They are both covering the lob so neither player closes enough to hit an effective volley. If you hit the ball cross court, you know you are the closer! Don't hit from person to person. This changes your duty every time (closer, stagger, closer, stagger). If I hit the ball down the line, I need to end the point, or my poor partner will have to change duties quickly and without warning.

Two Back

This should be the least effective of all the positions, but it really works. I see it all the time. Two ladies are getting crushed by a baby Serena and Venus, so they move back because they are tired of being human targets. So, they just push it in. Lob after lob to slow things down. The aggressive team keeps coming in but then they miss a few opportunities (remember that easy overhead) so then they start pushing the ball in. Before you know it, those two ladies lob themselves to a victory leaving baby Serena and Venus sitting on the bench, wondering how this happened.

Why did the aggressive team lose? They kept trying to power through the player that has moved 20 feet back. It's just not as effective to use power in that situation. Try using the angle or the short ball instead of your "yeah, I do CrossFit" muscles.

    ***Whenever you have two players in the same position, down the middle solves the riddle. All we need is one little moment of uncertainty (yours or mine?) and that ball will slip right through. ***

Seven

Doubles Formations 4 & 5

Me:"Today we are going to work on modified "I" formation
My Lesson:"Wait, was there an original "I"?"

The Standard "I" Formation

If you have watched any professional doubles on the television in recent years, you are very lucky. They don't cover a lot of doubles on tv. Even though most recreational (that's you and me) play doubles rather than singles, apparently, we watch singles more than doubles. Go figure.

Back to business…If you have watched some doubles on tv, you may have seen the net player crouched low to the ground straddling the center service line and their partner serving closer to the center of the court. This is known as the "I" formation. I spent a lot of my playing career in this position. By crouching down in this formation, I could go to either side of the court equally as fast and my partner could cover the other half. As a short person, this made me much more effective at the net when my partner was serving. I even flashed my server some signals. The first signal I gave her was where I wanted her to serve and the second signal determined which way I would move. Trust me, that is not as complex as it seems!

I tried teaching this formation for years with very little success. Most pairings were just not comfortable with this formation. I thought it was the net person who felt vulnerable or unable to pop up out of the crouched position quick enough. I started playing for the first time in over a decade, and I tell ya, I felt it in my knees when I was down there. But crouching down wasn't what deterred my partner from wanting to play the "I" formation, nor was it what made countless others that I was teaching uncomfortable.

It was the server who was uncomfortable. That's right. Not at all what I thought. Turns out, they were too nervous about hitting their partner in the back or the head (thoughtful group of ladies, aren't they!). One day I happened to catch some doubles play on the television and there it was. The net person was off to the side of the center service line. This allows players to serve without hitting the ball over their crouching and defenseless net player. In my day, we called this position Australian. However, when we did Australian, we didn't poach out of that position. We were there to cover the cross court return and/ or try and force them to return down the line. I now teach my players to poach or stay out of the modified "I". Call it whatever you like, but make sure you add this to your game plan.

I haven't taught regular "I" in couple of years now. Modified "I" is much easier to learn and apply.

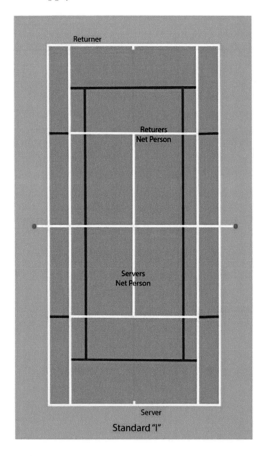

Modified "I"

The difference between modified "I" and standard "I" is the position of the net person. Instead of straddling the center service line, the net person just sets up to the left or right. They should be aligned directly in front of their server. Now the server has more room to serve and the net person is still in an aggressive position to pounce that return of serve.

What target do I have them serve to in this position? I have my ladies serve out wide. That makes for a full angle change for the returner if they try to hit down the line. If they can do it, great. You must reevaluate your target. If not, it will be a very long day for your opponent. I have my players agree on the service target verbally beforehand and when they get into the formation, give the signal as to which direction they are moving. Make sure as the server that you VERBALLY confirm that you see the signal. Your net person doesn't have eyes in the back of their head.

***A little extra bonus for trying out this formation...If you choose to stay as the net person in your original position it forces the rally down the line. Since the ball is travelling straight instead of at an angle, you have a better shot to poach because you can crowd that center service line. If you insist on playing one up one back, please try this and make your tennis life (and your coaches) much, much easier. ***

A second little extra bonus for trying out this formation...It could freak out your opponents

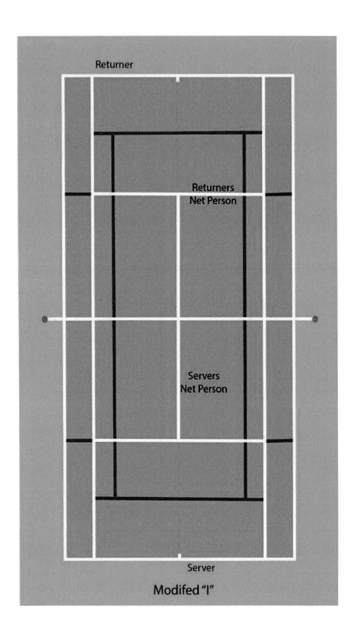

Modifed "I"

Eight

MY FAVORITE APPROACH SHOT

Me:"What do you do after you hit a good lob in doubles?"
My Lesson:"Watch it in all its glory"

The Lob Approach Shot in Doubles

This might be one of my favorite plays. The lob gets a lot of grief for being slow and some people go as far as to say the lob isn't real tennis.

That's because someone whipped your ass with it over the course of several, agonizing hours. Bitter much?

Whenever you lob over the net person, this is quite simply, the easiest approach shot that can be hit in doubles. You could walk in to the net after hitting this shot. Your position is everything here. Don't come charging in like you are about to lock horns. Hit the lob, then come up to the service line. Your partner should also shift back to the service line here. The biggest mistake people make in this case is the person at the net shifts closer to the net. That creates an opening behind team at the net. The easiest shot to hit off a lob is a lob! If one or both of you come crashing in and hang out on top of the net, you will get lobbed! This isn't rocket science people. If they are incredible lobbers, both of you take position one step behind the service line. If they suck at lobbing or they hardly ever lob, come in one step inside the service line. Adjustments don't have to be dramatic, but they do have to be made. Remember, you came in to win. This position will allow you both to cover your own overhead or move forward to hit the volley. Put that first ball away! That is your best opportunity to win the point.

Melissacious

If you get caught admiring your shot, you will then get caught admiring their shot.

Nine

ATTACKING THE 2ND SERVE

Me:"Adding power is the last way I want you to be aggressive"
My Lesson:"So, today's lesson is going to be no fun at all?"

The Weakest Shot in Tennis

I said it earlier and I will say it again, the 2nd serve is the weakest shot in all of tennis. Even on tour, where their second serves are better than most of our first serves, it is the most attackable part of their games. In our regular, adult playing, tennis world, it is the easiest shot you will get during the point to attack. While the server should be swinging faster to get more spin, most of us play it safe and "just get it in". The result is a ball that A) the returner knows where it is going to land (the service box!) B) the returner knows it's going to be slow and C) the returner knows they should win the point. As we all know, however, expectations can be killers. The last one is the one that gets us. It's like the easy overhead and you KNOW you should win the point. There is that whole mental thing, again.

Most players take this shot as an opportunity to come and kill the ball. Here is the thing, that ball has almost no pace. So, when you come up and "kill" it, you better have some mad tennis technique. One of the hardest things to do, and do consistently, is create pace on a ball that has no pace. You also have a shorter court to deal with, so you better add some spin. If you don't have topspin, this could create some serious consistency issues.

So, what do you do after you have hit the back of the fence and the bottom of the net a few times? Remember, power is not the only way to be aggressive. One of my first go to returns off this weak second serve is the drop shot or a good short ball cross court. The server is required to start off serving behind the baseline and is giving you a super slow and short ball to work with so this ideal for one of these little buggers. What is the difference between a drop shot and a short ball? A drop shot has a higher trajectory over the net and is really designed to be a winner. Ideally, I would clear the net by a couple of feet and the ball would bounce and die well within the opposite service line and the net. A short ball has a lower trajectory over the net. It's like you are hitting a short slice. The short ball is a definitely higher percentage than the drop shot, so if you struggle with finesse, this would be the route for you to take. Both shots are effective in this situation and will greatly affect the reaction of the server over the course of the match.

Once you establish that you can hit the drop shot or the short ball effectively, then you can lob over the net person if she is still there. The server is having to come in a few steps to cover that nasty little dropper, so that space behind her net person is big time open.

Her net person is pretty crafty, though. She consults with her partner, and decides rather than going two back, she will just back up a couple of steps to combat the lob so that her partner can cover the short ball.

It's like winning the lottery, people.

Now the middle of the court opens up like the Grand Canyon. You come up and hit a forehand or backhand at about 75% pace down the middle. Boo yah. The net person could technically get it, but they have a lot on their plate right at this moment. They have to worry about the lob, the line, getting their face taken off, that kind of stuff. Their mental state is pretty defensive at this point.

Not to leave this little gem out, this is a good opportunity to go down the line. This can be a very effective shot! Let me give you a little advice. Go right at the body of the net person. If gives you a big target in case you are a little off and, let's face it, fighting off a volley going right at your gut is a difficult shot, especially if you are still trying to hit that two-handed volley on everything or have the wrong grip. No, we are not trying to hit her. We are trying to make her hit a difficult volley. She chose to stay up there even though she knows her partner is serving total poop over the net. That's the price she will pay.

Going deep and cross court is still a viable option here, and if you are having success with it, go for it. You can catch the server out of position in no man's land trying to cover the short ball. It's just one more way to mix up your return patterns.

Ten

"THE GAME YOU SHOULD ALWAYS WIN"

Me: This game is called "The Game You Should Always Win"
My Lesson: "My self-esteem is suffering, here"

The Game You Should Always Win

I love this game. To me, it is one of the most useful games in the wom-
en's doubles world. Remember that whole "2 back" thing and the
mental collapse of the overhead? This game hits the nail on the head.

One team starts up in the middle of the service boxes and the other
team starts on the opposite end on the baseline. The two players on the
baseline can only lob, the two players at the net can only hit overheads.
The overhead hitters should win. Period. They are on the offensive; the
lobbers are on the defensive. Play to 11.

Here is where this game gets very interesting. The lobbing side wins, a
lot, and it usually stems from the overhead hitters trying to use power
instead of targets. It's not all about power! If you hit it a hundred miles
an hour to the wrong target, it will probably come back. If you hit it 50
miles per hour to the correct target, you will win the point. We covered
earlier about using the angle cross court instead of trying to drive it
down the line. If you establish the angle on BOTH sides, that middle is
going to be wide open. Down the middle solves the riddle!

Eleven

"THE POINT THAT NEVER ENDS"

Me:"This game is called"The Point that Never Ends""
My Lesson:"So, when does it end?"

The Point that Never Ends

This game can be used for sheer conditioning purposes. It can take a court sometimes 15 minutes or more to just play one game to 7 points. I like to use this game to show them the importance of hitting the target. If you don't hit the target when you get the chance, you could add a couple of minutes on to that point.

The Rules

The rules are simple. Teams take turns dropping and hitting to start the point from the baseline. All four players start at the baseline, but can go anywhere during the point. The balls' first bounce must land within the boundaries of the ENTIRE court. The ball can land outside the doubles side line and be in as long as it doesn't land on the court next to me on the first bounce. We have nice little seams that separate each of our courts, so we use those as our boundary markers. The ball can even hit the back or side fences first. If the ball is not rolling or has not come to a full stop, that ball is still in play. If the ball bounces within the boundaries of your court, but then continues to bounce onto the next court, that ball is still good.

Tons of strategy can be used here. You can lob the ball high enough and deep enough to bounce over the fence and out of reach. You can angle it making it impossible to track down. You can hit it into some side netting to make it roll. This is a great game to make your players think outside of the box. We learn the most when we go outside of our comfort zones. This game is also great for conditioning. The players usually don't notice how tired they are until the game or extra-long point is over. Such a fun game!!!

Side note, I don't let my players dribble the ball to the net. They can scoop, hit, or dribble enough to get themselves in hitting position, but they must hit from the first spot they can. Makes it more fun and fair

Twelve

DRILL: FOLLOW THE LOB IN!

Me:"Come in, come in, come in!"
My Lesson:"Did you see that lob?!"

Follow the Lob In!

This is a drill I have just hammered into the brains of all my team clinics. When you lob that net person, come into the service line!

Have the players stand one up one back to start (back players on the deuce side, net players on the ad side). Designate one of the back persons as the feeding position. This person feeds (or the pro can feed) the ball to the opponents back person and this person then lobs it over the other net person. If this lob sucks, the net person should nail that overhead. Make the back person hit a good lob! Once the lob successfully clears the net person, the lobber comes up to the service line and creates a wall with their partner in the same position and the point is played out. You can run this just as a drill or you can keep score to up the ante a little bit. Once you get the hang of it, switch it up and have the back persons on the ad side.

****Remember, if you aren't practicing your overheads, this drill isn't going to do you a whole lot of good. Make sure you are getting your reps! ****

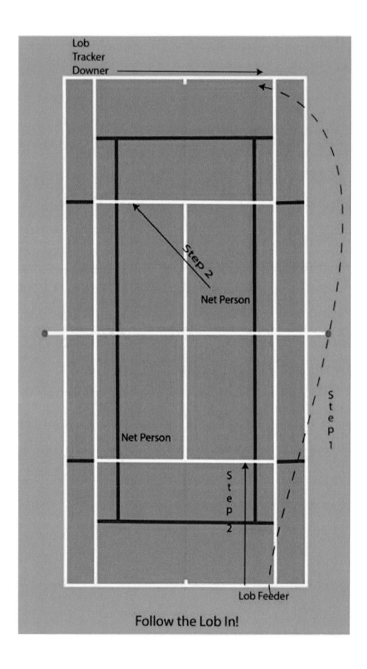

Follow the Lob In!

Melissacious

If you close your eyes, you won't see the ball hit you

Thirteen

KILLING THE HOPES AND DREAMS OF
EVERY OVERHEAD HITTER YOU MEET

Me:"How did you get hit?"
My Lesson:"Which time?"

Killing the Hopes and Dreams of Every Overhead Hitter You Meet

I remember getting totally nailed in the chest doing this drill in high school. Hope you enjoy it!

Start two overhead hitters up inside the service box and two players on the opposite service line. Feed a fairly easy overhead to the overhead hitters and have the other two players retreat while the ball is in the air. The trick here is to have them set up and get their weight forward right before the ball is struck. It is amazing how many balls you can get back if you are set and balanced! I like to go through the rotation once with a new group, then keep score the second time around. If you can just get one overhead back, you can start to chip away at the overhead hitters' confidence! I just love it when you can totally tell they are starting to get really mad because they aren't putting the ball away. Even better than that? When their partner is obviously pissed because they aren't putting the ball away. If you can get your opponents frustrated with one another, you are doing something very right!

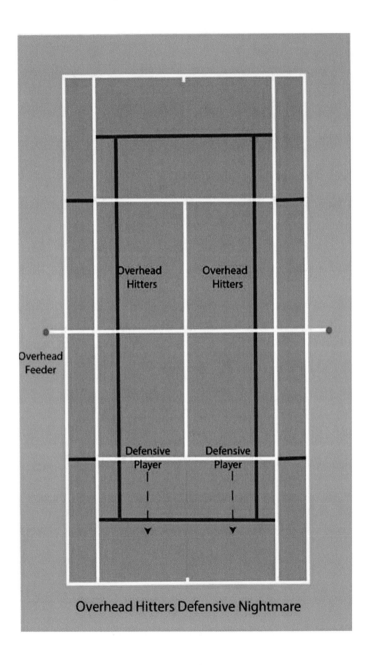

Overhead Hitters Defensive Nightmare

Melissacious

You are better off having better balance, than having better position without balance

Fourteen

*Me:"When your partner hits that first
ball down at their feet, poach"
My Lesson:"Are you freaking kidding me?"*

My Net, Not Yours

Whenever your opponent begins to approach to the net and comes in to join their partner, your back person has one shot to keep this approacher at bay. If you can roll the first ball crosscourt at their feet, your partner can poach this ball.

Have one up, one back on one end of the court and two up on the other end (net person cross court from the back person needs to start on the service line, other net person can be up a couple of steps in the box). Feed to the back person and let them work on getting the ball cross court at the approachers feet. The approacher is the person starting on the service line cross court from the player on the baseline. You can do this drill with the back person and the approacher on the deuce or ad. Whatever you want to work on. If you are feeling really frisky, do it from both sides!

We have a lot of things we are working on in this drill. The back person is working on getting the ball at the feet and the approacher (approacher is apparently not a word. My spell check says so) is working on hitting a volley or half volley hit at their feet. The big skill I want you to focus on in this drill, however, is the poacher reading the closing net person. If the approacher comes in with their racquet up high (they could crush you right here) the poacher should remain in their area and guard it to the best of their abilities. If the approacher gets pulled out wide, the opposite net person should follow that ball. If the approacher can't get any angle on it, it will just go right to the net person. But if you see that approacher bend down inside the singles court, this means this ball is right at their feet and they don't have as much angle to work with. The poacher should have eyes the size of saucers. This is it! Your moment. Take it. Right before contact, poach. Just cross to the other side and cut that ball off. If you are successful, great, if you aren't, that can pay dividends later in the match. Poaching is about more than a single point. It's about your opponent's knowing your willingness to poach. If they see you as an aggressive net person, they could end of making low percentage choices later to avoid you. That is a deadly weapon, my friend.

***Approacher, approacher, approacher, approacher approacher. Take that, spell check. ***

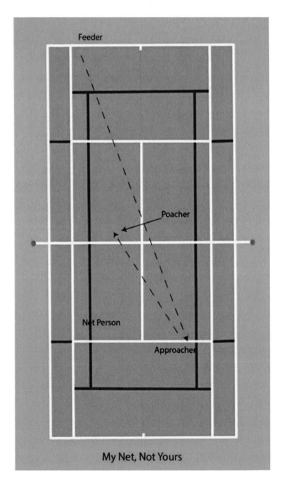

Melissacious

Wind-day is my favorite day of the week

Fifteen

WIND = WIN

Me: "The wind is your friend"
My Lesson: "I don't have very good taste in friends, do I?"

Wind=Win

As a product of West Texas tennis, I learned to love playing in the wind. If you have never played in this area, you truly can't appreciate what type of winds we are talking about. You could literally hit the ball sideways towards the next court and the ball could come back into the court of play. I am not making this up. I took a couple of friends of mine to Abilene a few years back and we decided to hit my old middle school courts for an afternoon of tennis. They witnessed for themselves one of these legendary wind days. My high school coaches did an excellent job of drilling into all of us that we should embrace those conditions.

The result?

I freaking love playing and coaching in the wind. I know I will win when I step onto the court and my hat blows off. I love hearing my opponents complain about it. It's like adding fuel to my competitive fire. I have tried to pass my love for this friend nobody wants on to my clientele. Every time it is windy, they think of me (probably not all good thoughts. Just to be fair).

How do you learn to befriend your former enemy? First, let's cover some basics. Believe it or not, it is easier to play against the wind than with the wind. When you are against the wind, you have a license to kill. You could just nail the ball and the ball will go in. You can also hit the ball super slow and watch the wind take that ball back towards the net and away from your frustrated opponent. One of my favorite plays is to hit a short ball into the wind. Give me a crosswind and I will totally ruin your day! Nothing says entertainment like two different winds to work with. Doesn't this sound devilishly fun????

Inevitably, you will need to hit with the wind. If you have topspin, just roll that ball about 6 feet over the net and aim for the service line and let the wind do the rest. The height on the ball is a key part of this strategy. By getting the height on the ball, it allows the wind to take the ball out of your opponent's strike zone. Once the ball is out of the strike zone, it will be difficult for them to get any depth on the ball because they are hitting against the wind. If you don't have topspin, you can still execute the strategy, just make sure you don't aim too high or too deep or the wind will put a pair of wings on that ball and fly it to the fence.

Wind-day Serving

I get asked this question a lot on those windy clinic days. Which server should serve with the wind and who should serve against the wind. Good question that could have many answers. Let's go over all the factors involved.

Your partner has a big serve. Most teams automatically put this player serving with the wind, so the serve can be bigger. This usually results in a lot of big serves going really long. I like to have this server serve into the wind. They can still crank out some mph's and their percentage should greatly increase. When they execute one of these big serves, it can also make returning perilous. If the returner tries to take a big crack at the ball, the wind will combine with the pace on the ball and launch that ball to the back of the fence.

But let's say your partner has a poopy serve. I also like this server into the wind. It's like hitting a short ball on the serve. Now, if you have a rainbow serve (I am a huge fan of this serve. It's like a kick without all the fancy spin) serving with the wind can be awesome. Just aim high and just over the net and let that wind pop that ball right out of the strike zone of the returner. If you have an actual kick or top spin serve, serving with the wind can be devastating to your opponents.

Communicate

They say the secret to any good marriage is communication. The same applies for doubles partners. Don't assume your partner is taking the wind into account. Talk early and talk often about the direction(s) the wind is blowing. You will be amazed as to what a difference it makes. Don't complain about it, communicate about it.

The Changeover…
The Kim Gidley Effect

I tell my students all the time "I'm not making this stuff up, people", and I mean it. I didn't invent tennis (and, if I did, the scoring would have been a hell of a lot easier) and I certainly did not invent its basic strategies. I do, however, think I am fairly decent at passing along that information.

So, who is the best coach ever? I really don't know the answer to that because I have not met every coach on planet earth, so I can only base my knowledge on those I have taken lessons from or worked with.

My nominee for this one would have to be Kim Gidley. I have taken something from every coach I have ever been around, but she is responsible for much of what I teach today. Kim has one wicked tennis mind. I remember her strapping on her knees and stretching herself out to her full five-foot height. Her game was a bit slow, but it was deadly. Her ability to construct a point was a wonder to watch.

Her ability to coach was and is even better.

She always seemed to have the right strategy. Even if that strategy was seemingly ridiculous, it worked. You could truly tell that she enjoyed coaching us, even though I know we sometimes made her feel like pulling her hair out. I don't think any of us at the time truly appreciated how lucky we were to have a coach of her caliber as our high schools' assistant turned head coach. Props to you, Gidget.

Sixteen

It's Getting Kind of Deep

Me: "You need to find good depth"
My Lesson: "It was in. Isn't that good enough?"

It's Getting Kind of Deep

Depth is a priority in tennis. Whether it's a drop shot or deep ground stroke, finding the right depth can be the difference between winning and losing the point. We are all so worried about power and creating openings side to side, we forget to add the correct depth. Here are a few drills and games that can help develop depth.

The Basic Deep Ball

Simple drill. You can play this half or whole court. The ball must land in no man's land to be in. If it lands on or short of the service line, it is out. Play to 11 (make sure to take turns feeding). Just because a drill is simple in nature, doesn't make it easy to execute. One thing you will notice during this drill is if you get the ball in the back half of no man's land (past the 10 and Under baseline) it makes it more difficult for the other player to get it deep back to you.

To Come In, or Not to Come in...

When do you come in? You can serve and volley. Come in on their second serve. Come in behind a high ball, that sort of thing. The easiest time to come in is when the decision is made by your opponent hitting you a nice, easy short ball. In this drill, if the ball lands on the service line or shorter, you must come in behind it. If it lands past the service line, you stay back. Yes, this is a very simplified version of when to come in, but sometimes we do better when we have fewer decisions to make. In this game, if you can keep it deep, you can keep your opponent back and increase the chances of them hitting you a short ball. You can play this half or whole court and play to whatever score you like or have time for.

Volley Depth

Power, power, power. Everyone wants more power. I get it. It is fun to hit hard. Like, really fun. It's usually not necessary, however, especially on your volleys. I stress this point every opportunity I can. Depth is a priority on the volley. If you hit it 105 mph and the ball lands out in front of your opponent, it comes back 106 mph and all they had to do was stick their racquet out and let your pace do the rest. On the flip side, you don't want them hitting the ball in the strike zone either. This is why technique and grips are so important. If you use the wrong grip or you love to take a big swing at the volley, it will be difficult for you to consistently find the right depth and keep the ball low out of the strike zone.

If you are looking to develop this consistent depth on the volley, try this little nugget. Hit 20 in a row service line to service line in the air. This sounds so easy, doesn't it??? Even my advanced adult players struggle with this one. This is one simple drill that can take you to great volley heights.

Tri-Ball

I love this one because it is so difficult, yet so rewarding. Tri-Ball is the execution of three shots: the serve, return, and first volley. This drill is executed crosscourt and includes the doubles alley. The server and returner are working together during this drill. To get 1 point, the server must serve and volley, hitting the first volley in the air past the 10 & Under baseline cross court (yes, it does have to be in!). I think the difficult position in this drill is the returner. You must hit a very precise return for the server to execute the deep volley. When you return, you are working on depth. That means you want the server hitting a volley above their waist. Spend some time on this one. It can be frustrating because it is difficult to execute, but can pay huge dividends during your matches. If at first you don't succeed, try, try, again. I bet you just rolled your eyes!

Seventeen

THE HARDEST DRILL, EVER

Me: "You did it! You took the ball on the rise!"
My Lesson: "Did I? My eyes were closed so I couldn't tell!"

The Hardest Drill, Ever

If you have done any clinics with me in the last decade and you saw the title of this chapter, I am fairly certain you just flipped me off. This is never a fan favorite, but it's one of my favorite things to work on.

The hardest drill ever will help you work on taking the ball on the rise (taking the ball on the bounce. Potato, Potato. That saying just doesn't really work when you type it out, does it?). I have one end of the court lobbing down the line or cross court. You need to lob this ball into no man's land. The other end moves up to the ball and tries to hit it immediately following the bounce. We hit on the rise frequently, we just usually do it defensively rather than offensively.

This drill might seem impossible to execute, at first, but it will get easier! Just look around at your team mates! That first time, you all might look like it is your first day of tennis! Keep at it. This can be a devastating shot.

When you take the ball earlier than your opponent, it disrupts your opponent's footwork rhythm. They hit a lob, so they saunter around without a care in the world and then, BAM! That ball is coming back way earlier than expected. This also beats the hell out of backing up 15 feet behind the baseline repeatedly and continuing the lob rally.

One of the side effects of working on this particular shot is how aware you must be of your foot work. You don't get to wait on the ball to come to you, you must go and get it! Being in position to hit this ball is the hardest part.

Over the years, quite a few of my clients have implemented this shot into their games. It is awesome to watch. Many times, their opponents don't even have time to react and the ball passes right by them.

***Once you get taking the ball on the bounce down with the lob feed, have your partner across the net feed you a regular ground stroke. This ball is much easier to read and take on the bounce. You will surprise yourself with how much pace you can generate with little effort. ***

Eighteen

Me:"Ok, let's play a tie breaker to 7, second serve only"
My Lesson:"It's like you don't want me to win"

Second Serve Only

It is pretty much impossible to duplicate the pressure of an actual match, but you should try and put yourself in as many pressure situations as possible when you practice. One of the drills we do to up the ante in practice is playing tie breakers with second serve only. This means you only get one chance to start the point. If you miss, it is a big, fat, double fault.

There is pressure on both sides of this serve, however. The returning team should win this point. The server is trying to keep her team from getting destroyed on the return. Can't you just feel the pressure???

There are many variations to this game and feel free to play around with the format. Sometimes, we let one team have first and second serves and the other team is second serve only. The team with both serves should win this one hands down, but expectations are killers. You can also give one team a substantial lead in the tie breaker, but second serve only or vice versa.

Feeling like you want to amp up the pressure some more? Throw down some lines or tape in the service box. Not only must the second serve go in, it must land in a specific target area. Pressure? Ha! You eat pressure for breakfast.

Nineteen

PRACTICING WITH A SILENT PARTNER

Me:"Have you ever hit against the
wall? It has never been beaten"
My Lesson:"That wall hasn't seen the likes of me"

The Wall and the Ball Machine

Do you have a crazy schedule? Can't really commit to a league or clinic? The wall and the ball machine were made for you.

These two amenities, found at most tennis courts and facilities, are grossly under used. These two trainers won't judge you. They won't tell you to just get it in. They will just keep that ball coming back over and over until you get it. A more loyal tennis friend you will not find.

The Wall

If you have ever hit against a wall, you probably spent a good amount of your time tracking down the ball in the north forty behind it. The wall may not judge you, but it can be very unforgiving. If you angle it just a little too much, it will bounce back out of your reach. If you open your strings, the ball goes over the wall. This is what makes it a very powerful training tool. If you keep at it, you will get so tired of chasing the ball that you will eventually get it right.

Start off simple with the wall. Pick a spot that feels like it is the equivalent of the baseline to the net on an actual court. Try to hit 20 consecutive ground strokes. Take it up a notch and just hit 20 consecutive forehands. Move on to the backhand next. Next, try and alternate forehand and backhand groundstrokes. Volleys? The wall can help with that too. You must control how much pace you put on this ball or that wall could give a tennis ball tattoo. See if you can hit 20 consecutive forehand only volleys. Then, move to the backhand. Now for the grand finale, see if you can alternate volleys. This is quite the challenge and achievement!

Overheads on a wall? It can be done. To start the rally, hit the ball down so that it bounces right before it hits the wall. This should pop the ball right up. Don't try to kill it. That ball will go crazy on you. This is designed to warm up the general motion.

Mean, Lean, Ball Machine

If you have access to a ball machine, use it! Ball machines can give you the reps you need to build muscle memory for all those fancy mechanics you work on in your lessons. Ball machines come in many shapes and sizes. Some can serve 100 mph at you, others can be programmed on your smart phone, and some are just capable of throwing a decent ball your direction. No matter how fancy the ball machine, it can help you take your game to the next level.

Most ball machines come with the same basic features. Ball feed, ball speed, spin, elevation, and oscillation. Ball feed is the time between balls fed your direction. Ball speed is how many miles per hour that ball is coming your way. Spin is just whether the ball is fed with slice, flat, or topspin. Elevation controls the height of the ball over the net and oscillation can pivot the ball machine left and right to give you a mix of forehands and backhands. Play around with these controls. You can set that ball machine up to feed you overheads, volleys, regular ground strokes or even slice opportunities. These fantastic machines can even give you 100 in a row drop shot opportunities. How is that for finding a rhythm?

Twenty

COMBO AND MIXED DOUBLES: DON'T COMPLICATE IT

Me: "Hit to the weaker player"
My Lesson: "Ummmm, yeah, that would be me"

Benching the Better Player

In recent years, I have had the privilege of playing combo doubles. Combo is where two players of different NTRP levels combine to create a level. An example of this would be a 4.0 and a 4.5 combining to form an 8.5 team. I learned so much from this experience that I began spending more time coaching and focusing on combo doubles.

Lesson number one: You are only as good as the weaker player. I could go an entire game and only touch the ball when I served or returned. My opponents essentially benched me during the point. If we won the match, it was because of my partner, not me. We had to rely heavily on modified "I" so that I might get a chance to poach or at least become more involved.

Lesson number two: Hit to the weaker player! Find her, no matter where she is at. Don't complicate this. No, you normally shouldn't go down the line, but you will now. No, you normally shouldn't hit to that target, but now you do. If you can break the weaker player, you win. If she can hold your own, you will need to branch out from this strategy.

Lesson number three: If you are the higher rated player, don't act like a jerk towards your partner. Even if she is the crème de la crème of her level, she is still a lower level player, so her skills aren't going to be as polished as your own. Your opponents are attacking her, constantly, and she is going to miss some. Cut her some slack. She is hitting most of the balls on your end of the court so of course she will miss more than you! I witnessed several of the higher rated players berating their partners, and that does not make the situation any better. Encourage, stay positive, and make sure SHE would actually want to play with YOU again. If my partner enjoyed playing with me, then I felt like we won no matter the what the outcome of the match was.

Mixed

Mixed is very similar to combo. The three lessons above apply here as well. I would like to add two more lessons to this one…

Guys, don't be a ball hog! It's one thing to poach and cover what is yours, but let that lady play, especially if she is better than you!

Ladies, if you stepped onto that court, you cannot complain about being hit at. Sorry, you aren't getting any sympathy from me. You signed up to play that level, so you knew what you were getting into. If you feel like you are being targeted, it's because they see you as the weaker player. It's not about your sex, it's about your ability.

Twenty-One

TALK IS NOT CHEAP

*Me:"What is a good example of
communicating during a match?"
My Lesson:"Yours!"*

Communicating Your Way to a Win

Communication is key in doubles. Making sure you are on the same page as your partner can be an unsung hero in your next doubles win. Don't assume that your partner sees the same things that you do. Is there a lefty on the other side? Is her backhand better than her forehand? Don't keep these little gems to yourself. Point these things out to your partner!

Communicating can be as simple as "Yours!" or "Mine!". It's the communication between points and on changeovers, however, that we sometimes neglect. Do you plan on returning down the line? Your partner needs to know this! If you return the ball down the line and the net person gets the ball back, it will more than likely go right at your poor net person! Are you going to serve and volley? Tell your partner so they know you won't be at the baseline to track down a lob.

One of the mistakes I have seen teams make over the years is they only come together and communicate when they want to change something. Hello! Your opponents will catch onto this. You and your partner should come together between every single point, no matter how brief. I don't care if you tell them you want a beer, communicate every single time. Is talking about a beer ideal? No, not at all. But at least your partner now knows you aren't focused one damn bit because you really want a beer. You two might be on the wrong page, but you are on it together.

This next one is a big emphasis for me. Whenever you change ends of the court, whether it is the 90 second changeover or switching ends during the tie-breaker, go with your partner. If you go around one net post and she goes around the other, you have wasted valuable communication time with your partner.

Is everything going wrong? Is the broad side of a barn too small of a target for you or your partner at the moment? Sometimes you will walk on to that court and have an outer body experience. Like your mind is willing but your body isn't able. You will just suck and so can your partner. Communication can be key here. Say something funny. Keep it light. Stressing out about it will only make it worse. Sometimes, we do better when we don't take it so seriously.

No matter what level you are at, communication is something you can be good at. It doesn't take topspin or control to execute. You don't need to be a 5.0 to communicate, you just need to be willing to talk about what is going on in the match.

I feel like you owe me an extra fifty bucks for the therapy session…

Ladies, the 90 second changeover or set break is when you should be making your plans for the next point and/or game. When that break is over, you should be ready to play! One of my biggest pet peeves is when players come together for a long conversation about strategy immediately following the changeover. Make the most of every break and you can decrease the amount of time wasted on court!

The Changeover…
Time is of the Essence

Time is Money

I am a very on time person. Actually, I am always early. I don't like to feel rushed and I try to maximize every hour of my day. I wasn't always this way. I made many mistakes in my early career. I procrastinated, rescheduled and cancelled an embarrassing amount. Father time has honed me over the years and experience has made me appreciate what some of my clients go through just to make it to that one -hour tennis lesson. Some of my clients are always late. That is their privilege. They paid for that lesson and they can be late if they want to.

Your pro needs to be early and prepared every time. If they are constantly late or cancelling last minute, dump them. They don't deserve your business.

Tennis lessons are a luxury. Yes, they make you better and can help you fulfill your tennis hopes and dreams, but they aren't clothes or a car or wine (wine is a necessity, like air). They are something you spend your extra, hard earned money on. Your pro should appreciate this. The fact that so many people want to drop over $50 an hour to learn from me is something I don't take for granted. I make a living teaching something I love, and I am grateful for that.

I understand that emergencies happen and occasionally, something occurs that just won't allow your pro to be on time. This will happen to me a few times a year. If this is happening every week with your pro, you need to move on to someone who thinks enough of the income YOU provide and who will be there with bells on and a few minutes to spare.

Cell Phones

Your pro should not have this on the court. It is a distraction for the pro and their client. Does your pro use it to keep time? Get a freaking watch. Do you need to take a quick video of your client and show them the serve in slow-mo? Shoot the video on their phone if possible. If you must use your phone, put it away after you are done where you can't see it or hear it. Even on silent, you can still see that little screen light up and that is a distraction. I am also not a fan of a pro wearing a watch connected to their phone. If you must wear one, disable any features that could distract you during the lesson. You need to be 100 percent present during a lesson. Your client pays you handsomely for your time. Devote that time to your client and only your client.

Twenty-Two

5 Balls to a Better You!

Me:"Make her hit 5 balls"
My Lesson:"I think that is what she is
doing to me. It really works!"

Just Five Balls...

Sometimes, we just need to get a rhythm. Other times, we make our strategy too complicated. And, as we discussed earlier, sometimes we just suck it up. Whether you are playing singles or doubles, I always thought this was a very simple yet effective strategy. Make her hit five balls no matter what.

I remember my coach Kim Gidley giving me this advice early on, and it stuck. If I was super nervous, I would remind myself of this strategy repeatedly. Just make her hit five balls.

You will be shocked at how effective it is. Most of our points are relatively short, five balls or less. We remember the epic, long points so vividly because there aren't that many of them.

You can use the whole court or half court for this drill. Flip a coin or spin a racquet to determine who gets to do what. One player only must make her opponent hit five balls and she automatically wins the point. Play to 7, or 11, or whatever you feel like. Switch duties the next game.

What you will quickly notice is that you don't get to enforce that five-ball rule very often. A mistake or a winner ends the point before you get to the magic number most of the time.

If your opponent only has to make you hit five balls to win the point, it means you must go for more on the third and possibly fourth ball. This adds an element of pressure to execute that is so vital when we practice.

Twenty-Three

THE SKUNK GAME

*Me:"What's your biggest enemy on the
tennis court, other than yourself?"
My Lesson:"100 percent, without a doubt, that damn net"*

Something Stinks, and it Might be my Tennis Game…

Ah, the net! The big demon that stands in the way of your mighty victory. Ok, that might be a little overkill, but you have to admit, tennis would be a heck of a lot easier without it. I have heard that if you never hit the ball into the net, you would automatically make 25% fewer errors (more or less). That's an absolute game changer. Think how many more matches you would have won if you made 25% fewer errors?

This game is called the Skunk Game. This is going to require some math skills, so pay attention! Each point is started by dropping and hitting. Alternate turns feeding every two points and play to 11. Now comes the math part…

If you hit a volley or overhead clean winner (clean winner is a ball that bounces twice before being touched) you get three points. If you hit the ball in the net (or it doesn't make it to the net) you go back to zero. Brutal. All other points won are worth one point. If your opponent hits it wide or deep, it's just one point won.

If one of you can get to a score of 7(or more) to 0, that is a skunk and you automatically win. I love this game. It is so mental!!!! Imagine being up 6-0, on the cusp of victory, and dumping the ball into the net. Now your opponent is up 1-0. So close, yet so far away. Are you winning 4-0? If you came to the net, you could end this game in one shot. My favorite scoring position is when both players get their score to seven points or above. The pressure not to hit the ball into the net is thick in the air. Both of you are getting closer to 11, so you still must try to win the point. This is a game that can make you so mentally tough, you could spit nails.

Twenty-Four

THE DOMINANT SHOT GAME

Me:"Footwork is the key to consistency"
My Lesson:"Well, that explains a lot, doesn't it?"

How to Dominate Your Lazy Footwork

If you stopped improving your strokes completely right now, how could you ever get any better? Learn better footwork. Footwork is not about getting to the ball, it's about getting to the ball, so you can hit the ball in your strike zone as often as possible. If your footwork improves, every shot you have ever worked on will automatically get better.

This game is called the dominant shot game. There is some strategy to this game and will give you reps on either your forehand or your backhand, but I like to use it to make my lessons more aware of their footwork.

How to Play

Play the point cross court using the alley. Drop and hit alternating turns feeding every two points and play to 11. Oh, and just one more thing...

You are only allowed to hit the dominant shot. The dominant shot is the stroke closest to the alley. If you are right handed, the forehand would be your dominant shot on the deuce side and the backhand would get the title on the ad side. If one player is forced to hit the wrong shot, they automatically lose the point. For example, if I am on the deuce side hitting my dominant shot, I lose if I hit a backhand (I am right handed). If you decide to come to the net in this drill, you must still use the dominant shot. If you are supposed to hit forehand ground strokes, you must also hit only forehand volleys.

One thing you will notice while playing this game is how awkward it is to run around and hit backhands only. If you avoid your backhand like the plague, this is a good drill to force you to hit as many backhands as possible. This is what you have always dreamed of, right?

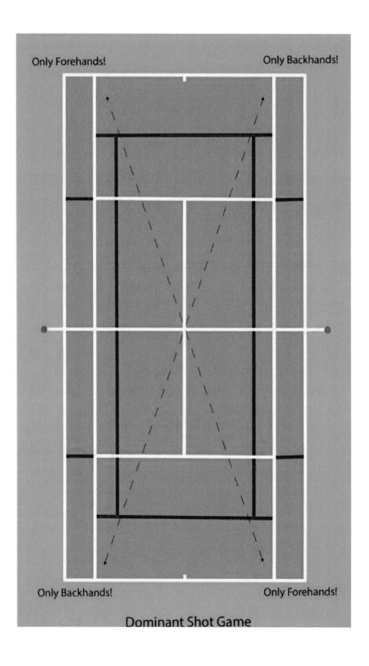

The Changeover…
Negative Nelly's are Not Necessary

The Power of Positive Coaching

No one expects our coaches to be happy with us all the time. They should see what we need to work on and let us know about it.

Sometimes, they may even have to get a little stern with you. I have had to go there a time or two myself. However, I firmly believe if you must yell and degrade a client to get your point across, you might be in the wrong profession. It's just tennis! The world did not end because she didn't come in behind that lob or because she didn't loop before that forehand. It's just something you must go over again and again because that is your job.

I have had clients tell me before that their tennis lesson is personal therapy time. It's one hour all about them. One hour to think about something other than Jimmy's failing math grade or that last minute presentation at work. It's one hour to not think about the pressures of life. Make that hour a positive experience. Make them feel better about their day, their week, or even their life. It's just tennis, but it's not just a tennis lesson.

Twenty-Five

THE BACKHAND SLICE: THE LIFE JACKET OF TENNIS

Me:"You can dig your way out of trouble
with a good backhand slice"
My Lesson:"I don't think you understand
how deep that hole is"

Backhand Overboard!

Now that you love that crushing two-handed backhand of yours, why should you even bother learning a backhand slice? When you chose that two-handed backhand over a one hander, you chose easier to learn and taking the ball earlier over the ability to reach. Don't beat yourself up over it. You made the right choice! A good backhand slice can help you overcome this lack of reach.

What is slice? Slice is a spin that rotates back towards you as the ball travels towards its target. The result is a ball that stays low to the ground after it bounces. This bounce keeps the ball lower than the ideal strike zone for your opponent and forces them to hit up which gives you more time to recover. Sounds pretty damn useful, doesn't it? It is!

We are going to cover the backhand slice. There is such a thing as a forehand slice and it can be useful, but with that two-handed backhand, you will see many more opportunities to slice the backhand. The backhand slice preparation is just like the preparation on that one handed backhand volley.

1. Racquet head eye level
2. Tip of the racquet head pointed toward the top of the fence behind you
3. Racquet head should be slightly tilted away from your face

Now, you are ready to slice. Keep your wrist completely locked when you swing forward to contact. You will step and hit on this shot since you are swinging high to low. Step with the right foot as you make contact. Make sure your contact point is out in front of the right foot. Stop just past the contact point.

Ok, it's time for the "f" word again, footwork. Immediately following contact and the step with the right foot, swing your left foot behind your right foot (kind of like a curtsy!) then let that right foot kick out again. You do all of this while still holding that racquet just past the contact point. This footwork isn't as complicated as it sounds, and it will make learning the slice much easier. If you can execute the footwork, it will give you natural extension through the swing and keep your shoulders turned towards contact. What does all this mean? It means a better slice for you!

When would you have to use this shot? Anytime the ball is hit low to your backhand or stretches you out so far that you can barely reach it is a great time for slice. If you really put some time and effort into learning this shot, it can become a weapon for you. Your opponent thinks they have hit a winning shot and you not only get to it but hit a great, deep slice to reset the point. Trust me, this can frustrate your opponent to no end. If your opponent must keep hitting a better shot to beat you, their percentage of getting the ball in play starts going down and the percentage of you winning goes up.

***If your opponent does not have a backhand slice, your backhand slice could be a big problem for them. It is difficult to get low enough to hit a good ball with a two-handed backhand and a good slice could put them in this difficult position more times than they can handle. ***

Twenty-Six

GETTING HIGH WITH PERCENTAGES

Me:"Play the percentages"
My Lesson:"I suck at math"

Percentages, smentages

I go over percentages quite a bit with my clientele. I think they are an invaluable tool to understand why you need to do certain things in tennis. Like I said earlier, I'm not making this stuff up. I don't make you do things, so I can look back at it later and have a laugh with my pro buddies (or do I?). That backhand slice you just learned? It greatly increases the percentages of you winning that point even though your opponent just hit a great shot and pulled you out of the court.

You can never cover everything. No matter how fast or experienced you are, part of that court is always open. Part of playing the percentages is understanding this. Your goal when you cover the court is to only allow your opponent to hit the low percentage targets. That tiny angle that is open when you crush the net? If she hits that, good for her. Awesome shot! You gave her that tiny target and she executed. Can she execute that shot over and over again? Doubtful. That's playing the percentages.

I have some bad news for all you tennis players out there. No matter how much you train or how good you get, you can never predict how well you will play a match. Sometimes, you are just on fire. I could throw a nickel on the court and you could hit it every time. For every one of those days, though, there are the days when you couldn't hit the broadside of a barn. It happens to all of us. I like to tell my clients I want them to play ok and win. Not awesome. It's too difficult to be awesome all the time (I know a few of you will argue that point!). Just focus on playing within yourself. Don't worry about all the cool stuff she can do, just worry about what you can be consistently capable of. This is the 75% you. This is not you maxing out your abilities, it is you doing what you KNOW you can do.

The 75% you means not trying to nail every serve, but maybe serving 75% of your power level. The 75% you is more likely to choose higher percentage targets and strategies. The 75% you is more likely to win.

When you watch professional tennis on television, pay attention to all those stats they post. Percentage of first serve points won and lost. Percentage of first serves in. Percentages don't lie. If those percentages are low for player A and not the player B, the percentages of winning the match are lowered for player A as well.

***Have you ever had one of your matches charted? Probably not because it sucks to be the person charting it. If you do have a friend or spouse that has nothing better to do than pay attention to your tennis game, ask them to chart it for you. You can download charts from the internet and I am sure there is an app floating around out there. If your BFF says, "hell no", then your record your match and chart it yourself later. Some clubs and facilities have cameras available and mounted for just this purpose. You can also rig a camera up on the top of the fence or curtain behind the baseline. I promise you, it will be a game changer for you. ***

The Changeover…
The Terminology Conundrum

The Right Words Matter

Down the middle? What does that mean on a tennis court? It literally means down the center of the tennis court. Now, picture yourself serving. Your partner says, "Serve it down the middle" and you are immediately confused. Did she mean serve it down the middle line or serve it in the middle of the box?

The correct terminology IS a big deal. It can save you a lot of unnecessary confusion. Let's cover some of the biggest terminology blunders I see.

Let's start with serving targets. Repeat after me: Out wide, in the body, and down the "T". There is no serve down the middle. You know that "just get it in" serve your partner wants you to hit? The terminology for that is "in the body". Sounds a lot cooler when you say it that way, doesn't it?

"We volleyed back and forth like 20 times!" What did you picture? Two people up at the net hitting volleys back and forth. That is exactly what I pictured! This is not what they meant. They meant to say they hit 20 groundstrokes in a row. A volley is a shot taken in the air, a groundstroke is hit after the bounce, typically baseline to baseline. You could also refer to this baseline exchange as a baseline rally.

This is big one for me. Don't cover your alley, cover your half! If you tell your partner to cover their alley, that is exactly what they will cover. The result is them leaving the other half of what they should be covering open. You know this feeling. It is totally your partner's ball at the net and it goes right by them and you are left standing there taking the blame. If you are playing the deuce side, cover the deuce side, not just your alley!

Twenty-Seven

*Me: "Watching that singles match was
like watching a 2-hour warmup"
My Lesson: "So, what did you think?"*

This One's for You

I can't leave this drill out. For all of you singles players out there (you are like finding a diamond in the parking lot!), this drill is for you.

Put some throw down lines or tape half way between the singles side line and the center service line. Extend this all the way back to the baseline. If you have enough lines or tape you can extend the lines all the way to the net, but if you don't, just try to imagine that extension.

Drop and hit, alternating every two points. Play to 11. The only special rule is the ball cannot land in between the lines you laid down. That's it. You must hit it in the court of play and outside the special lines.

This drill is a game changer for most singles players. It really brings to their attention how often they actually hit down the middle. I'm not saying you should never hit down the middle. There is absolutely a time for that. But none of us should hit down the middle as often as we do. It's a safe play and it is easy to get sucked into the black hole of safety. Yes, you are more likely to get the ball in if you hit it in the middle. It would be the highest percentage play. The downside of it is you just gave her the same thing. She can now play right back down the middle (no angle change involved here). It's like you are dueling until the death, and it is a slow, agonizing death. It is for your coach, anyway. I don't care how fit you are. If it is 100+ degrees on the court and your team is counting on you to play four singles matches that weekend, that type of play will sink you.

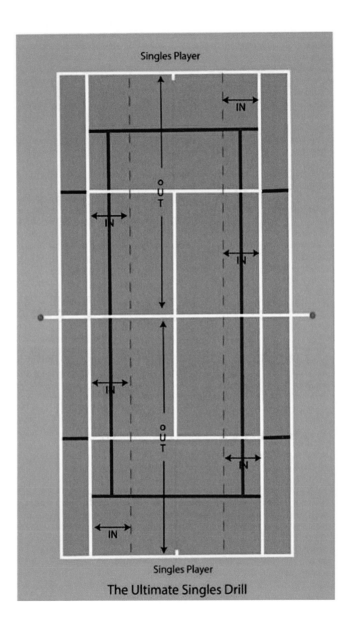

Twenty-Eight

DISCOVERING RECOVERING

Me:"You have to recover"
My Lesson:"How did you know I was hungover?"

Where the Hell am I?

That's a pretty good question, isn't it? What we are referring to is your position on the court. Knowing your position on court is vital to making good decisions. How many of you have a habit of volleying while you are standing just inside the baseline? You hit it because you weren't aware of where you are in the court. Learning to recover correctly is a big part of this.

Where should you recover after you hit a ball? Depending on where you hit the ball, this could vary your recovery position some. We will start basic. In general, in doubles, your recovery if you are staying back (chicken!) is within a foot or two inside the singles side line and about a foot or so behind the baseline. In singles, you recover a couple of feet behind the baseline and behind the center mark (that little hash mark that separates the court into two halves).

When would you adjust these positions? Let's say you hit a killer angle in doubles. Remember, angle creates angle. Your recovery position should reflect this. After you hit this angle, your recovery position should move closer to the singles side line in doubles and to the left or right of the center service mark in singles. We aren't talking huge adjustments; the adjustments are subtle but effective.

The Split Step

This is the single most important piece of footwork you need to have. Many people tell me they don't have time to split step. I tell them they don't have time NOT to split step. What is a split step? It's a decision step. Right before your opponent strikes the ball, you take a balanced hop with your legs shoulder width apart. Even if you don't make it to your recovery position, you need to split at this moment. You are better off having better balance than better position without balance. This step will balance you. Why do I call it a decision step? While you are in the air, you decide what is happening. Where your opponent is hitting the ball, which or how much spin, how hard, that kind of thing. When you land, because you are perfectly balanced, you can explode into any direction. Watch the pros. They split every single time without even thinking about it. I tell my clients if they never change another thing about their strokes, if they improve their footwork, they will go up another level. Adding or improving a split step is the first piece of footwork you should tackle.

Twenty-Nine

HOW TO SERVE AND VOLLEY LIKE A BOSS

Me:"You have to serve and volley or you lose the point"
My Lesson: (First Point) "Crap, I forgot!"
(Second Point) "Crap, I forgot!"
(Third Point) "Crap, I forgot!"

Charge!

The serve and volley is not dead. Did you hear me? Singles or doubles, this is still a very useful play to make! I realize serving and volley can be rather daunting, but it can pay huge dividends over the course of a match. Do you have a huge first serve? Many times, your opponent will just float the return back just to get the point started. This would be a great time to serve and volley! If you serve and volley a few times, it puts more pressure on your opponent to hit a better return. The better the shot they must hit, the more errors they make!

We are going to cover the serve and volley in doubles. Most adult players are going to be more comfortable with this play in doubles rather than singles, so we will please the masses.

First things first. Don't wait to see if you have hit a good serve to come in and volley. You know before you step up to the line that this is your plan. Make it or miss it, you should already be a few steps inside the court by the time they return, or your ball hits the net or lands out. Second, don't make a beeline for the center net strap. This will make you coming forward at too much of an angle. If you are serving from the standard doubles position, come straight ahead until you reach the service line, then angle towards the net strap.

Third, remember not coming in like a wild banshee??? This is a huge deal when you serve and volley. Split or balance when they strike the ball, no matter where you are in the court. No, your position may not be ideal, but if you are balanced you will have a better play on the ball.

***It looks easy on tv, because it is easy on tv. I say this to my clients all the time. The pros look graceful coming towards the net. They don't look like a wild animal charging its prey. Balance, balance, balance. ***

Thirty

THE MIDDLE IS A BUSTED PLAY

*Me:"You know what it's like to play with
someone who "kind of" poaches"
My Lesson:"So does my partner"*

Meet Me in the Middle

If you still insist on playing standard one up, one back even after reading this fabulous book, this chapter is for you! I emphasize this play with all my teams early on, so they can take advantage of, or get out of, this situation.

We all know what it's like to play with someone who "kind of" poaches. They act like they are going to poach but they don't really, and you end up trying to react quick enough to hit the ball you thought they were going to hit. This is bound to happen to all of us sometime, but some players make a real habit of acting like they are going to poach. This can be very frustrating for the player on the baseline, especially since most of the balls land in the middle of the court. When the ball lands in the middle, I call it a busted play. When the ball is in the middle, the opposing net person can follow the ball, placing them more towards the middle of the court and making it more likely they can poach. This puts the opposing baseline player in a pretty sticky situation.

What should the player do at this point? Most of the time, they try to angle it away from the would-be poacher. The problem with this is, if they are successful, it creates an angle for the baseline player on the other end of the court. Now, the player who hit the ball is out of position trying to cover the middle and an angle has been created. This spells major trouble! A lob is your best and safest play here. It will give you time to recover back towards the alley and will not allow that pesky net person to poach.

The Middle Drill

Start players one up, one back. Have one baseline player feed a short ball inside the service box cross court to the other back player. This back player will come up and crush the ball down the middle and play begins. The first time you run through the drill, take the lob option away from the defending back person. Force them to try to angle the ball away from the net person. This will give the approacher a chance to put the angle that has been created away to open court. Next time though, allow the defender to lob or angle it away. The lob will keep that net person at bay and catch the attacker in no man's land.

If you can learn to spot this play in a match, you can really wreak havoc on your opponents. This is a must learn for all of you who insist on staying one up, one back!

The changeover...
Teams and Mates

Teammate, or Team monster

Do you have trouble with team sports? Are you not a team player? Do you cause problems on every team you are on? Not only do you suck as a person, but you are missing out on one of the greatest experiences you can have. Being a teammate.

I have had many teammates over the course of my life. Some good, some bad, some lifelong friends, but all still hold a special place in my cold and tiny little heart (that's some honor!). I remember junior high like it was yesterday. Practice after school every day and then hitting with Robbie or Paula afterwards in our quest to be better. High School? That was another level of comradery. We did everything together. We cheered each other on, made jokes and nicknames that still come to memory to this day. Winning was nice, but having each other's backs was the best part.

College teammates is not something that a lot of athletes get to say, but I did, and I am grateful for it. I went to two different colleges and got to know two wonderful groups of ladies. If any of them called me up and said they needed anything, I would drop everything and help.

Let's not forget the teammates I have acquired as an adult player. I have met so many wonderful people this way. For years, I taught tennis but did not play. It wasn't until I a couple of years when I started playing again that I felt like I truly understood the team dynamic and what it means to these adults. They aren't getting paid, no endorsements coming their way, and no college scholarships to be awarded. Don't get me wrong, they love to win. Who doesn't? My favorite thing is watching one of my teams lose and then go have beers together. No kidding. Anyone can be happy and up for a few beers or bottle of wine after a big win. That's an easy one. To get together and rehash a losing match and LAUGH about it? That's what teammates are really there for. They pick you up when you are down, good naturedly give you shit about losing, and share the experience with you.

If you aren't this person, you are missing the big picture. If you were teammates with them for just one spring season, you are a teammate for life. If they tell a funny story about that team you were on together 20 years ago, you will probably come up in the conversation because you were a teammate! Don't be the one who demands to play with so and so or won't play with Jenny because she isn't very good. Be the person on the team who will play with anyone, because you are being a good teammate. In other words, be a good teammate, not a team monster. See what I did there?

Acknowledgements

Where on earth do you start? To everyone I have ever worked for, worked with, played for or played with, thank you. I have learned something from all of you. I especially learned from the ones who corrected me when I was wrong or was just being an idiot. If not for you, I would still be making the same mistakes and I would probably not still be in this business.

My family. I wouldn't be anywhere without them. They have been my support for these long, tennis years. I remember one of the first times my mom came to watch me play in high school. It was a pretty tense moment. Tied 4-4 in the second set, her ad, against my arch nemesis, and my mom yells "Smile, Melissa!" Better coaching advice, I have not heard. My dad taking me out to play for the first time. I remember being in awe of the fact that he could actually play! He had me swinging for the fence. Thirty minutes later, he had created an absolute tennis animal. If you don't like the book, you can just blame my dad. My older sister, Laura, has become my best friend in life, but we didn't always get along growing up (remember the can opener and the broken window?). I remember my sister showing up in her cheerleading uniform when my high school team climbed out of the bus after winning a state championship. Now, I am sure they were required to be there, but she looked genuinely thrilled that I won. That was the best part about winning state. Hands down. To my sister, Samantha, thank you for showing me how to use a compass and open a can of refried beans with a nail and a hammer. I feel I could survive anything. Raymond, you are the ultimate sports fan and I am the ultimate fan of you.

To my friends who have tolerated my tournament weekends (working or playing), special events or workshops, midseason or state tournaments, thank you so much for sticking by me. I can go months without seeing your smiling faces, so it's nice that you let me back into the club when I have been such an absentee friend. Stacey, Tim, Luke, Brandy, Jeremy, Shane, Taylor, Holly, and Meiling, you are all the best friends a person could hope for.

I can't forget Western Arkansas Tennis Association (WATA) for going along with all my crazy ideas (most of them have worked!). Ms. Jackson, Marge, Kami, and Dawn, it's been a hell of a fun ride! I know my roller coaster is always changing directions, so thank you for holding on and coming along with me. I couldn't have done it without you. You are what takes my dreams and helps makes them a reality.

To all my clients over the years, thank you from the bottom of my heart. You might be paying me to teach you tennis, but over the years I have learned just as much from you (no, I will not pay you for this). I am proud of all you have accomplished on and off the tennis court and look forward to many more years of listening to inappropriate comments, dirty jokes, and waiting for some people to respond to a group text thinking that it's just me texting them. I am so lucky to have a job where clients turn into amazing friends. To all of my juniors, don't think I don't love you! You are the greatest bunch of kids on planet earth and I am privileged to be a part of your tennis careers. Some of you will go on to play collegiate tennis or beyond, but you all will be able to play this amazing game for the rest of your lives. That is what I am most proud of. A special shout out to everyone I have played combo or regular team with. You ladies are awesome. Every win we had was because of you.

This last line is for all my ladies I teach daily,

"You said balls!"

41747135R00075

Made in the USA
San Bernardino, CA
05 July 2019